Empowered,

Empowered, Resilient and *Uniquely* YOU!

CHERYL A.S. HURLEY

Empowered, Resilient and *Uniquely* YOU!

DEDICATION

This journal book is dedicated to every woman who desires to treasure her profound learning experiences and use them to empower other women. Each one of us can reach another.

Empowered, Resilient and *Uniquely* YOU!

Introduction

First and foremost, I am humbly grateful for the small, still voice of our Creator who has and continues to challenge me in so many areas of my life journey. Only Abba Father knows how to stir up our inner desires and passions, which ultimately are used for His purposes. By chance, despite what you may have experienced or are experiencing now, do you realize that you were made on purpose for a purpose? Well, you were!

While I have several areas of giftedness that are used to encourage, inspire, and empower individuals, I had a secret passion I struggled with for many years. That passion was writing. You might ask, 'why did you struggle with it?' I proudly grew up in the Mantua section of Philadelphia during an era of gang wars and families in crisis. I learned firsthand that the struggle was as real then as it is today. In high school, I was assigned to a Motivational Counselor (Career Advisor) whose role was to encourage youth to consider college and tap into their area of interest. I enthusiastically went to her office one day and said I recognize what I want to do as we were preparing applications to various colleges. I shared with her I wanted to be a journalist. Do you know what this leader who was supposed to inspire young people said? And I quote. 'Cheryl, very few people of color are successful as journalists and perhaps you should consider becoming a Social Worker.' Can you imagine the look on my face? I was astonished at her perceived knowledge and thought, wow, that's amazing! I guess I'll just settle with being a Social Worker and that's exactly what I did. I was a very effective Social Worker because empowering others is one of my passions and purposes. Yet, I still had an unfulfilled longing to write.

This and other life experiences have enhanced my perspective on leadership as being a three-dimensional transformational approach that focuses on mindset, wellness, and heart. As you read through each chapter, it is my intent you will be empowered and embrace both your resilience and the power of operating from a growth mindset that shapes your heart as a woman of purpose.

Empowered to Inspire!

Cheryl

Empowered, Resilient and *Uniquely* YOU!

ACKNOWLEDGMENTS

~ SPECIAL THANKS ~

Annie Lois Simmons Reginald Sullivan Hurley, Sr. Reginald Sullivan
Hurley, Jr.
Shannon Tiffany Hurley
Jayden Charles Simms
Gloria Jean White
Pamela Elaine Nichols
Dr. Veirdre Ridgley-Jackson
Joanne McCrae
Rabbi and Pastor Cynthia Dobson
Dr. Robert Earl Brown
Pastor Linda K. Brown

These individuals consistently encouraged, guided, and had great faith in my
abilities. Your unwavering love and support is immensely
appreciated. I love you to life!!!

Empowered, Resilient and *Uniquely* YOU!

CONTENTS

Chapter 1

Women Who Lead

"It is this belief in a power larger than myself and other than myself,

which allows me to venture into the unknown and even the

unknowable". - Maya Angelou

Women in leadership – what a powerful phenomenon! Throughout history, the social and legal status of women has fluctuated despite the severe and vicious discrimination some have suffered. From the 18th century until the present, women in civilized lands have experienced collective education and the right to vote. Through the impact of their beliefs, they are equal with men in the great achievements of education, art, literature, social services and missionary activities. Specifically, women have been valuable and continue to make great contributions. Women in leadership are to be applauded for their tenacious commitment in using their spiritual gifts, talents, and abilities to be dynamic agents of change.

Despite the deserved applause, there were times on my journey to leadership where I felt I failed as a leader. While failure is good, my thoughts derived from the many facets of formal and informal encounters devoid of ethical values that govern healthy decision-making. During these tumultuous experiences, I was often challenged to abandon my assignments out of sheer frustration and might I add intense anger. I asked myself, 'how can they do this? What are they thinking?' And last, 'why is this happening to me?' I later learned that each experience - no matter how painful – was a significant part of my leadership shaping.

When I reflect on women in leadership, the faces are too numerous to mention and I salute them all. Yes, we can collectively look across the spectrum and identify many making a difference and affecting lives immensely. While I am grateful for their respective accomplishments and the differences they are making, I am also reminded of a very simple portrait of women in leadership. These women are making great contributions to their families, communities, workplaces, and within their circles of influence. Their character shines beyond the titles they hold and their greatest accomplishments. Let's consider these characteristics and how they portray the power of a leader.

1. **A Woman of Faith** – a woman who recognizes there **IS** a supreme being greater than she and understands the necessity of spiritually pacing herself for her divine journey. Therefore, she takes moments to call upon, meditate, and seek guidance in executing the navigation of her assignment.

2. **A Woman of Hope** – a woman who recognizes the need for encouragement not only for others but also for herself. Therefore, she embraces the art of self-care, taking quiet reflective moments to regroup, reassessing and inviting inspiration as a key ingredient during her divine journey. Women in leadership are reminded of taking moments to be still and be confident during this journey and remain steadfast knowing that **ALL** things work together for those who love Abba Father and the called according to His purpose. Leadership is a calling!

3. **<u>A Woman of Wisdom</u>** – a woman who recognizes the need to seek and use wisdom effectively. As Kathleen Norris is quoted, a woman of wisdom understands that 'before you begin a thing, remind yourself that difficulties and delays quite impossible to foresee are ahead…you can only see one thing clearly, and that is your goal.'

As women, let us not make the mistake of minimizing or devaluing our various leadership roles. Whether you have been called to lead a nation out of adverse conditions, your family out of poverty, or lead a campaign to legislate for a cause that could turn the world upside down, your character plays a

> # Wisdom
> # Pearl
>
> She is clothed with strength and dignity, And she laughs without fear of the future. When she speaks, her words are wise, and she gives instructions with kindness.
>
> *Proverbs 31:25-26*

vital role in your ability to lead powerfully and positively. Let's take a quick glimpse at a powerful woman named Esther.

Esther is the woman who saved her people from genocide. Esther is revealed as a woman of unambiguous judgment, outstanding self-discipline, competency, and of the noble self-sacrifice. Esther's character reminds us of the magnitude in seeking divine guidance in times of complexity and challenge. As leaders, adversity doesn't denote that we abandon our divine assignments but become *Women of Faith*. We also discover that obtaining knowledge of human character aids in our ability to know how to take advantage of any circumstance we face which may favor our cause to grow to be *Women of Wisdom*.

Last, we acquire the way of thinking that Esther is known throughout history for. Her assignment was clear, she unquestioningly accepted it and made the decree without hesitation or reservation as a woman of tenacious commitment by her illustrious quote, *"And if I shall perish, I shall perish!"* Esther's attitude in making this bold approach is courageous as she was determined to be obedient to her divine assignment, no matter what the cost.

Each of us –including **YOU** - has the potential to be a tenacious committed leader in our environment. Never take too lightly the power you possess but embrace it completely as it will make an encouraging impact.

Resilient Affirmation

I acknowledge that I AM POWERFUL

I acknowledge that I AM EXTRAORDINARY

I acknowledge that I AM AUTHENTIC

I acknowledge that I AM RESILIENT

I acknowledge that I AM GOOD ENOUGH

REFLECTION ACTIVITY

Which characteristic as described resonates with you and why?

_____

_____

_____

_____

_____

_____

_____

_____

What life learning experience was a major contributor to your leadership shaping?

_____

_____

_____

_____

_____

_____

My personal empowerment chapter reflection...

_____

_____

_____

_____

_____

_____

_____

_____

_____

_____

_____

_____

_____

_____

_____

_____

_____

_____

_____

_____

_____

_____

_____

_____

_____

_____

_____

_____

_____

_____

_____

_____

_____

_____

Chapter 2

Women Overcoming Obstacles

Reflection…Meditation…Silence…Appreciation

Each of these words, reflection, meditation, silence and appreciation exemplify empowerment. As we move about in such a hurried society, we must acknowledge that we are encompassed with many expectations and needs. If we are not careful, we may develop a tendency of overextending ourselves, which creates barriers to our divine purpose and destiny. It is and always will be my belief that within each of us lies a seed of greatness. Yet, if we don't learn when to say "no" enabling us to activate the discipline of solitude, we rob ourselves from the ability to experience empowerment.

I recall writing this chapter while sailing across the Eastern Caribbean. The ship was amidst much excitement and activity and people were having lots of fun. While I can appreciate the value of laughter breaks, I have also come to appreciate and embrace the power of creating inner peace and serenity. Do I like many of you have challenges and barriers to fulfilling my purpose? Of course I do! However, creating inner peace provides opportunity for us to channel our thoughts from the obstacles, barriers, and challenges to one of empowering stimulation.

Life is filled with many challenges and unexpected events which consist of economic hardships, illness, family circumstances, broken marriages, substance abuse just to name a few. The list goes on and on. But these are real life challenges we all have and will experience in our lives. I recall a low period where it seemed as if nothing was going right and was chaotic. And I mean nothing! I found myself frustrated, angry and becoming hopeless. On several occasions, I found myself stressed, wallowing in self-pity, and overwhelmed asking 'Why is this happening to me?' It seemed that the more I focused on the situations, the bigger the obstacles

> # Wisdom Pearl
>
> YOUR life purpose is empowered when YOU abandon self-defeating distractions and give intentional focus to unleash YOUR personal greatness.

became. Notice I said, 'focused on the situations.' I soon learned that I had relinquished my power to whatever I allowed to captivate my mind and my thoughts. I had allowed myself to become captive to everything external to me rather than unleashing the greatness that lay within me. When I recognized there was nothing I could do about the things out of my control, I learned to change my thoughts about my circumstances and strive towards fulfilling the purpose divinely placed upon my life. As I decided to trust divinity, I learned that I didn't have to go through life trying to figure things out. Instead I consciously decided to allow myself to develop. While on my journey to discovering my purpose, I established four empowerment tools, which consist of these disciplines:

1) **Reflection**: Instead of giving attention to the obstacles that hinder, we can create a visual of our purpose and direct our focus to what needs to be removed for us to be productive, liberated and successful.

2) **Meditation**: Mediate on that visual until it becomes insatiable and becomes your reality.

3) **Silence**: Instead of the noisy impediments that may threaten one's ability to hear, dare to be silent so you may clearly gain spiritual guidance with clarity. Dare to have an **ear** to **hear** what YOUR **heart** is saying.

4) **Appreciation:** Accept and appreciate your selfworth and realize that **YOU** matter. Without question, **YOU** are uniquely designed with a purpose.

Women, it is time for you to abandon focusing on your challenges or the time it may take you to get from point A to point B. You must begin a paradigm shift to invite positive energy and healthy spiritual thoughts. I charge you to break the barriers of what is comfortable and take a leap of faith that will skyrocket you to becoming the person YOU were destined to be.

Resilient Affirmation

I acknowledge that I AM POWERFUL

I acknowledge that I AM EXTRAORDINARY

I acknowledge that I AM AUTHENTIC

I acknowledge that I AM RESILIENT

I acknowledge that I AM GOOD ENOUGH

REFLECTION ACTIVITY

As you reflect on empowerment tools, what paradigm shift was necessary for you on your journey of purpose?

_____

_____

_____

_____

_____

_____

_____

Do you recognize the value of incorporating Meditation, Reflection, Silence and Appreciation when facing life challenges?

My personal empowerment chapter reflection...

Chapter 3

A Woman's Red Sea Experience

"And it came to pass, when the people were removed from their

tents, to pass over Jordan, and the priests bearing the Ark of the

Covenant before the people;"

Joshua 3:14 (Emphasis mine)

Mostly, many of us are familiar with the story of the Israelites

being led by Moses to cross the Red Sea. Specifically, they were being

led out of captivity into the Promised Land. Let's look at their experience.

They were placed into captivity under harsh and cruel conditions. Now,

bring those same experiences into the present day. Some of us are in

captivity in our minds, homes, jobs, addictions, finances, and places of

worship. Day in and day out, we receive the same old treatment. During

the Israelites' time, The Master appointed Moses to tell Pharaoh to let

His people go. Today, we have an advocate who continuously interceded

on our behalf.

The previous chapter dealt with overcoming obstacles. One, which requires that you pay close attention to is trust. Imagine being prompted by the Spirit to raise our trust to the level of where we are in our NOW and saying let go and see changes happen. When you think about it, it's like a partnership being formed. Real, genuine, and unadulterated trust which challenges you to evaluate past situations to determine whether our Sovereign Master has ever failed us. When we reason rationally, we find that He has never failed

Now look at the word "**removed**." Removed means to take off, set aside, or do away with. The Scriptures states that 'He will never leave nor forsake us'. When referring to removed, we are referring to stepping out of doubt or fear into a "realm of trust." Now imagine again the Red Sea and visualize the Master telling you to prepare to cross over. We cannot do what He desires for us to do if there is unbelief, which indicates a lack of trust.

As the Spirit has led me, I believe that a person's mindset is comparable to that of a tent. Tent in the Webster Dictionary is described as a *moveable shelter consisting of material stretched over a supporting framework.* Now look at the framework as being a basic system of

28

arrangement, as ideas or thoughts. Where do thoughts originate? They originate in the mental bank otherwise called the mind. The mind is in our "human" framework that governs our thoughts, perceptions, feelings, will, memory, and imagination. Mindset is described as *a fixed mental attitude that predetermines our response to and interpretation of situations.*

As we make the connection in this analogy, the tent is being compared to an individual's mindset. Trust is necessary in its greatest form so that you can completely move out of self and walk in His precepts and trust Him. We must step out of ourselves and step in Him. Philippians 4:13 states that "I can do all things through Him who strengthens me..." Only then can we make the moves He requests of us without wavering or experiencing a strong doubt. It is therefore essential in the life of women walking in faith to understand and comprehend with "full" clarity of what is means to trust the Master.

Psalm 23 is a very familiar passage that demonstrates Him a Shepherd. What an awesome shepherd He is! One who guides, leads, and directs His sheep through green pastures. When I envision removing from the "tent of my thoughts" "my abilities" and "my strength" I recognize that without Him I can do nothing. But when I completely lean on and put my trust in "the Shepherd" only then can I cross over any situation. Listen to what it means to really see Him as Shepherd.

Abba, my Shepherd! I don't need a thing.
You have bedded me down in lush meadows,
You find me quiet pools to drink from.
True to your word, you let me catch my breath
And send me in the right direction.
Even when the way goes through Death Valley,
I'm not afraid when you walk at my side.
Your trusty shepherd's crook makes me feel secure.
You serve me a six-course dinner right in front of my enemies.
You revive my drooping head; my cup brims with blessing.
Your beauty and love chase after me every day of my life.
I'm back home in the house of Abba Father for the rest of my life.
(Psalm 23, The Message Bible)

When we look at the situations we are in or have been in, it requires trust parallel to that of the Israelites when they were asked to cross over the Red Sea.

It doesn't matter how zealous you are, you must possess the ability to believe in a power of greater authority. Trust Him to guide you through the storms of life without being defeated. In our many situations, a Red Sea

Wisdom Pearl

To do the impossible we must be willing to yield to the possible.

Experience is essential for us to see Him "moving" in our situations working it out for **His** good.

When we see Him working it out, we are no longer bound but made free to be who He called us to be, walking in the spirit of truth. Our situations no longer look bleak because we have been empowered by our trust in the Scriptures. This spiritual empowerment assures you that the Master will provide guidance and satisfy you during times of scarcity. You shall be like a tree planted by the water and called the repairer of the breach, the restorer of paths to dwell in.

Habakkuk's Prayer

Abba Father is my Strength, my personal bravery,

and my invincible army; He makes my feet like

hinds' feet and will make me walk [not to stand

still in terror, but to walk] and make [spiritual]

progress upon my high places [of trouble, suffering,

or responsibility]!

Habakkuk 3:19
(Read Habakkuk 3:1-19)

I recall several red sea experiences that challenged my faith. At age 6, my Mom and Dad separated and unbeknownst to me that began my struggle with family separation. At 16, the matriarch of our family – my grandmother died. I was devastated! I had no idea of anything except excruciating pain. I struggled with strong emotional pain. A few years later, I graduated from H.S. and attended college. There I got my firsthand experience with independence and learned early on that it was no joke. There I met my love and we later married. Four years later, we were expecting our first child. During our early years of marriage, we struggled financially, and I struggled with submission. I couldn't fathom someone telling me what to do, how to do it, and when to do it. So, I struggled with trust.

While still pregnant, my father was dying from cancer. I tried to be excited about the pending birth of our child, but I was often shaken by the fact my Dad was dying. It was a high-risk pregnancy and at six months, I was put on bed rest. At the seven month mark, my Dad died. Of all the days to pass away, he chose (I thought) Mother's Day. This was a heavy load – a second struggle with emotional and physical pain.

Prior to this, I saw the manifestation in my life of a genuine passion for those who were in need or hurting. While I had an excellent rapport at a local hospital, with my ministry family and friends, I continued to struggle with trying to find "me." I attended a worship service and for the "first" time, heard a message that while it convicted me, it challenged me to get real with myself. Suddenly, I recognized that I was simply doing what was expected of me and it was not meeting the needs in my life. I began to sense that Abba Father wanted more and it was time for me to open up and earnestly and whole-heartedly trust Him for guidance. I wanted to learn what His purposes and plans for my life were. This began a major transition in my life. My taste for the things I thought had meaning diminished and I was developing a genuine hunger for the things of the Master. I was spiritually psyched and then BOOM - my sister dies because of leukemia. Boy, was I made mad at Abba! How dare He, I thought, take my sister. I blamed Him as I hadn't grasped 1 Corinthians 15:51. So, my anger was misdirected, but boy, did He have a plan for my life. I experienced more emotional struggles.

As I continued to serve people in whatever way I could, it seemed as though I experienced various trials and persecutions I could not understand. While going through this and trying to gain understanding, my husband was ordained as a Deacon. As his wife, I became a Deaconess. I felt the need to apply myself in the word. I attended Bible Study, Sunday school, and later taught New Members Class. I traveled to conferences and was introduced to many facets of ministry. This coincided with my struggle to find "me." I have always been in search of "me" – no longer wanting to be who someone else thought I should be – but becoming who Abba Father said I was. This search resulted in many disappointments, rejections, and let downs by individuals who I held in high regard. I struggled financially and personally. I struggled with making a change from self-confidence to becoming confident in our Creator. I struggled with shutting out everyone else telling me who I should be and concentrating on that still voice who knew exactly what He wanted of me. As I stopped struggling and simply let go, I heard Him speak.

'He reminded me of the plan that HE had for my life – that I serve His people and minister whenever and wherever He opened a door for me to do so. He told me that my mouth no longer belonged to me but it was a channel for His truths to be spoken. He reminded me that my thoughts were to be subject to His and line up with His spoken word over my life. My hands were no longer mines but to be used to touch lives. My feet were to be directed wherever He sent them. He let me know that it was now time for me – His daughter to come forth. He reminded me of the many times that I had gone through, endured the pain, and that it was the time for me to fulfill the assignment that He has planned for me with all authority and effectiveness'

I no longer struggle but allowed my red sea experiences to be the channel to becoming the woman of purpose and destiny designed on purpose by the Master!

Resilient Affirmation

I acknowledge that I AM POWERFUL

I acknowledge that I AM EXTRAORDINARY

I acknowledge that I AM AUTHENTIC

I acknowledge that I AM RESILIENT

I acknowledge that I AM GOOD ENOUGH

REFLECTION ACTIVITY

As you recall YOUR Red Sea Experiences, what were some areas YOU were challenged with trust and why?

_____

_____

_____

_____

_____

_____

As you began or are in the process of 'letting go', what do you sense you are being guided to?

_____

_____

_____

_____

_____

_____

_____

My personal empowerment chapter reflection...

_____

_____

_____

_____

_____

_____

_____

_____

Chapter 4

Women Empowering Women

"We receive His peace when we ask Him for it.

We keep His peace by extending it to others.

Those are the keys and there are no others."

~ Marianne Williamson ~

As you journey through time, you will discover many instances of exceptional women who embraced their giftedness, talents and abilities toward many causes. Their labor of love was not just merely opportunities to serve only as advocates for women but also to empower women to better their communities and the world in which they live. In reflecting on women who have made major impacts and/or extraordinary contributions through cultural, religious, business, political, educational, entrepreneurship, or social service initiatives, the list was astounding.

Some of these 21st century women include such unparalleled pioneers like:

• Rina Amiri is committed to visiting diverse villages to improve the lives of women in whatever means she can.

While recognizing that the basic rights fall into four main categories that include education, health care, economic participation, and political participation, she is sensitive to the needs of the Afghan women. This sensitivity has channeled her energies by forming a women's media collective and mobilizing women to prepare for the Afghan Grand Council, which selected the current Afghan government. Rina Amiri states "I feel my ability to have an impact is absolutely minuscule, If I'm able to help one life, sometimes that's all it's about."

- Bushra Jamil is saluted for her tenacious determination in declaring messages of expectation and encouragement to Iraqi women living in difficult times. Despite the violent bombing of the radio station and the deaths of two staff members, this courageous woman is even more determined to continue her radio station broadcast.

- Aloisea Inyumba and Dena Merriam are an awe-inspiring team of women who together have made immense strides in encouraging peace and cooperation of women on both community and global levels. In reflecting on their astonishing contributions, Ms. Merriam unites women from around the world bringing together efforts and peace-building activities. After the Rwandan genocide, Ms. Inyumba helped to advance relations between Hutu and Tutsi women and their economic status and welfare through developing the Rwanda Women's Initiative.

- Phylicia Rashad is woman dedicated to humanitarian efforts including a commitment to improving the quality of life of economically disadvantaged people all over the world. Ms. Rashad is an active supporter of the PRASAD (Philanthropic, Relief, Altruistic Service and Development) Project, an international charitable organization that assists communities around the world through a wide range of programs in health, education, and sustainable development and disaster relief.

- Marisa Rivera-Albert is noted for her passion to compassionately instruct young Latina women to increase their leadership skills and ascend to roles of authority in commerce and administration.

- Susan Weidman Schneider, a noted writer is recognized for increasing the consciousness of the issues facing Jewish women via the media and her untiring support to young women.

- Dr. E Faye Williams is saluted as Chair of the National Congress of Black Women (NCBW). Founded by the late Honorable Shirley Chisholm, NCBW is dedicated to the educational, political, economic and cultural development of African American Women and their families. In her gentle yet positive, powerful and convincing voice, Dr. Williams leads the organization's mission to serve as a nonpartisan voice and implement on issues pertaining to the appointment of African American Women at all levels of government, and to increase African American women's participation in the educational, political, economic and social arenas. NCBW provides opportunities for women in leadership and decision-making positions in government, nonprofit organizations and the private sector.

It is my profound belief that within each woman lays a seed of greatness. For women to continue to empower other women, we must follow the steps of our forerunners who understood and embraced their divinely given purpose. All people have a purpose to demonstrate a commitment to the value of diversity, a passion to endeavor to bridge cultural gaps within the community, a purpose to promote cultural awareness, and understand and appreciate diversity.

Wisdom Pearl

Arise, for it is YOUR task and we are with YOU; Be Strong and do it.

Ezra 10:4

As we celebrate these and other women who have made and continue to make a difference, consider yourself. A glimpse of the late Coretta Scott King reveals a woman of greatness and resiliency hailed as the First Lady of Civil Rights. Her belief was that when you are willing to make sacrifices for a great cause, you will never be alone. Mrs. King summed up her and her husband's struggle by saying: "By reaching into and beyond ourselves and tapping the transcendent ethic of love, we shall overcome these evils. Love, truth, and the courage to do what is right should be our own guideposts on this lifelong journey."

Women empowering women!

Resilient Affirmation

I acknowledge that I AM POWERFUL

I acknowledge that I AM EXTRAORDINARY

I acknowledge that I AM AUTHENTIC

I acknowledge that I AM RESILIENT

I acknowledge that I AM GOOD ENOUGH

REFLECTION ACTIVITY

What is your purpose in life? Why do you exist? What is your mission?

_____

_____

_____

_____

_____

_____

_____

_____

_____

_____

Who were the women that most inspired, motivated, and challenged YOU on YOUR journey of purpose?

_____

_____

_____

_____

_____

My personal empowerment chapter reflection...

_____

_____

_____

_____

_____

_____

_____

_____

_____

_____

Chapter 5

A Balancing Act: Women Pursuing Higher Education

"Courage is the most important of all the virtues, because without

courage you can't practice any other virtue consistently. You can

practice any virtue erratically, but nothing consistently without

courage." Maya Angelou

In this fast-paced society, we must consider the many roles that women have. Some people ask this question – Who has time to study? It is typical for some to assume that most individuals complete high school, attend college, matriculate, secure that impressive position, marry, initiate a family and live happily ever after. Sounds great, doesn't it?

While women have made great progress in the labor force, there remains the need for advocates to make known the value of higher education because it increases the feminine movement in the labor force. This movement can effectively promote the potential to overcome the wage gap between women and men as well as reduce dependence upon welfare and unemployment.

There are many complex issues that in some instances have become barriers for higher education. These barriers include but are not limited to educational costs, inadequate need-based financial aid, poor childcare resources, and policies fashioned under the welfare reform. To add to this list are "life" experiences such as the demands of a challenging job, an ailing family member or the lack of financial resources all of which can become very stressful. These all too often have resulted in some women deciding to either postpone or abandon their pursuit of higher education.

During a quiet, reflective moment, I pondered the plight that some women have experienced to pursue higher education. I believe the consensus would reveal that there are challenges women from all diverse backgrounds and cultures have and will continue to face in pursuit of higher education. After we have individually and collectively studied the facts, arguments, and statistics these challenges will become even more prevalent. In addition, I am reminded of an important question that many women have pondered with higher education, which is affordability. The balancing act depends upon your perspective of the financial barriers you may encounter or making a choice to believe within yourselves that you can achieve academic success in spite of.

A spiritual route says, "Whatever I have, wherever I am, I can make it through anything in the One who makes me who I am." Despite your age, background, ethnicity, or the barriers faced, there is an apparent need to exercise audacity in pursuit of higher education. Further reflection reminded me of a testimony of praise I witnessed at my son's college graduation. The class valedictorian was a woman who had a physical disability, was married with three children, had seven grandchildren, attended college over an enormous span of time and had to take several breaks due to challenges with her health. She gave one of the most stirring orations of the importance of courage and determination. With every

Wisdom

Pearl

I can do everything through Him who gives me strength.

Philippians 4:13

painful step she took, the audience was stunned at her strength and quiet determination as she made her way to the podium. As she paused between breaths of overwhelming joy, she shared her most memorable

51

reflections and encouragement to the audience of not allowing anything to stand in the way of one's pursuit of higher education. As many of us were there to witness the graduation ceremonies of our sons and daughters, we also witnessed the tenacity and strength of seeing a woman who dared not to allow anything to bring to a halt the progress of her personal academic journey.

Today, I extend accolades to the many women who have pursued higher education. To those who may be at a crossroad of making a choice, I encourage you to make a difference for yourself, your children, your sisters, and other women in your circle of influence counting on you to open doors for those following in your footsteps.

"Invest in the human soul. Who knows, it may be a diamond in the rough", as Mary McLeod Bethune is quoted.

Resilient Affirmation

I acknowledge that I AM POWERFUL

I acknowledge that I AM EXTRAORDINARY

I acknowledge that I AM AUTHENTIC

I acknowledge that I AM RESILIENT

I acknowledge that I AM GOOD ENOUGH

REFLECTION ACTIVITY

What empowering beliefs can you take on to help you achieve your goals?

_____

_____

_____

_____

_____

_____

What were the manifested outcomes for you?

_____

_____

_____

_____

_____

_____

My personal empowerment chapter reflection...

_____

_____

_____

_____

_____

_____

_____

_____

_____

_____

_____

_____

_____

_____

_____

_____

_____

_____

_____

_____

_____

_____

_____

_____

_____

_____

_____

_____

_____

_____

_____

_____

_____

_____

_____

Chapter 6

Gifted, Talented, Skilled, and Empowered Women in the Arts!

"The elephant never gets tired of carrying its tusks."

-Liberian Proverb.

Never get tired of the things that make you the beautiful person you are. Your tusks (individuality) are the very things that allow the rest of us who recognize your worth to marvel at the very presence of you. There are times in your life when the world's hunters will try to attack you. The weight of life may be heavy on you, sometimes even cumbersome to carry. Never lose the essence of who YOU are for anyone.

Gifted - having great natural ability…

Talented – the natural endowments of a person…

Skilled - having acquired mastery of or skill in something…

Empowered – the activation of self-actualization or influence of…

Women are such phenomenal creatures...created with divine purpose...tenacious endurance...resilient women expressing themselves through the arts. I take delight in the numerous occasions I observed women exhibit their gifted skills in the arts. Their multi talents were in the form of creative and sacred dances, moving solos, heart-felt psalms, folklore, writing or painting on canvas just to name a few. These are reflections of artistic expressions.

In my personal and passionate plight to encourage and empower women, one area I coach women is taking their very own life experiences and transforming them into teachable life experiences. Sometimes during our life experiences, we can become distracted from our creative side hindering our ability to invite inspiration into our circumstances. The inspiration I am referring to is that component that taps into your creative artistic ability.

One way that I express myself artistically is through writing. When I go back and read some of my writings, I am completely in awe of the power of the pen. I have also been blessed to encounter women who have created soul-stirring lyrics or spoken-word, choreographed breath-taking dances, or artistic expression through abstract art.

One individual was diagnosed with a very serious ailment. She had a choice to make – to live in fear of the unknown or to take this profound life experience and channel it into an artistic expression. She made the choice! This woman opened the door to inspiration and found something that she could put her teeth in. Without ever knowing it, there was a gift – she was empowered with a natural ability to express herself through abstract painting and never knew it!

How many of us have been gifted with a natural ability? The answer is, ALL OF US. I encourage you to ask yourself whether you have taken the time to invite inspiration into your life to ensure that your artistic side is not lying dormant. Can you imagine that writing that someone needs to read, that dramatization that someone needs to experience, that song that someone needs to stir them, and that painting that speaks to the core of our being?

Women are creative and have been favored with various artistic expressions. Whatever YOUR expressions are, please know there are those whose spirit needs to be touched by YOUR gift! Dare to tap into your innermost being and discover that hidden talent. Let it be as dynamic to others as it is for you. Remember my belief, 'within every women lies a seed of greatness' – let it come forth.

I'm counting on YOU to create something artistic that only YOU can matchlessly design!

YOU are simply blessed and HIGHLY favored!

Resilient Affirmation

I acknowledge that I AM POWERFUL

I acknowledge that I AM EXTRAORDINARY

I acknowledge that I AM AUTHENTIC

I acknowledge that I AM RESILIENT

I acknowledge that I AM GOOD ENOUGH

REFLECTION ACTIVITY

Imagine three years from now and create an image of what you designed based upon what has happened to YOU both personally and spiritually.

_____

_____

_____

_____

_____

Of YOUR life experiences encountered, what was the greatest life lesson that has become a teachable moment you can share with other women?

_____

_____

_____

_____

_____

_____

_____

My personal empowerment chapter reflection...

_____

_____

_____

_____

_____

_____

_____

_____

Chapter 7

Fierce and Fabulous Women

I didn't know my own strength, And I crashed down, and I tumbled

But I did not crumble; I got through all the pain

I didn't know my own strength, Survived my darkest hour

My faith kept me alive, I picked myself back up

Hold my head up high; I was not built to break

I didn't know my own strength

Excerpt from Whitney Houston's I Didn't Know My Own Strength

.

Ladies – You are Loved! You're Fierce! You're Fabulous! You're Resilient and You're Uniquely YOU! Can I confirm it? The late Whitney Houston's song, 'Didn't Know My Own Strength' is so timely for this season, especially for women ready to experience a level of greatness despite the many challenges we face."

I have been compelled and inspired to speak life into YOU. My sisters there is undiscovered greatness within you! Psalms 139:14 reminds us that we are Fearfully, Wonderfully and Marvelously made in His likeness. The greater the challenges are in your life, the greater the victory will be.

Each of us has our own unique life experiences that sometimes cause us to forget our strength. However, we are made by the Master who is intimately familiar with our unique frame and we can rest assured that we have NOT been designed by the Master to break but to stand and be unwavering. In the spring of this year, I experienced yet another challenge – my health. I was speaking with a student and said to myself, 'I feel like I am about to faint and I did. I hit my head on a slate floor, suffered a severe concussion and was rushed to the hospital. A medication I was taking caused me to become dehydrated, my potassium, which should have been 3.9, was reported at 2.4 and my blood pressure was horrific. During my hospital stay, I had tests taken. Coincidently, a carotid aneurysm was discovered. This all occurred three days before I was to graduate from Eastern University. I was placed on bed rest, a modified low-sodium diet, and given a new medicine and required follow-up with a Vascular Surgeon. As I recall this period, I felt as though I was having an out-of-body experience but able to look in and ask, 'what in the world is going on?' I remain thankful for the prayer intercessors that lifted me up in prayer.

In early June, I had to have an ultrasound to evaluate the carotid aneurysm. While lying nervously on the exam bed, the technician questioned the location of the carotid aneurysm as she said, 'I don't see anything.' After probing, she called in the Director of Radiology who took over and continued the exam. He said, "We just completed a bilateral ultrasound and we don't see an aneurysm. We will send the report to the Specialist you are scheduled to see on June 29th." All I could say was 'HALLELUYAH!'

I retrieved the radiology studies from previous visits and reported for my visit on June 29th, 2017. While still somewhat nervous I went in faith and saw the Vascular Specialist. Upon examination, he reviewed all the reports and said, 'Mrs. Hurley, there is no carotid aneurysm.' I left his office in humbled awe praising Abba Father for the report. Again, all I could say was 'HALLELUYAH!'

I'd like to share three (3) points, on why we can boldly acclaim we are Fierce and Fabulous!

1) As Women, it is important that we walk in a spirit of faithfulness that is resilient. Specifically, no matter what confronts us we must keep bouncing back in pursuit of our unique greatness and teaching the women around us to do the same.

2) Second, we must embrace our fierceness or fearlessness as you will, with a spirit of tenacity. As we shared in Chapter 1, *Women Who Lead*, Esther was a tenacious woman whose mission to petition on behalf of her people caused her to cry out, 'If I perish. I perish." We too have been empowered to not be stopped or easily give in.

Last, we must embrace the fact that we are Fabulous because we are marvelously made. When we walk in this level of confidence, we fully accept that we are fearfully, wonderfully, and marvelously made in His likeness which means we are a force to reckon with.

Wisdom Pearl

YOU are BEAUTIFUL, FEARFULLY and WONDERFULY made!

Psalms 139:14

Shortly after my recent health challenge, I experienced some challenges that almost broke the very core of my being. I questioned the demeanor of some of my contemporaries, a great lack of ethical integrity I encountered and a resurfacing of that infamous question – 'why." As you will recall, we have already discussed that our experiences are a part of or leadership shaping. I am grateful that I have been blessed with those who speak life into me, encourage me, hold me accountable, and help me stay true to myself. One person, Dr. Veirdre Ridgley-Jackson (Vee), shared three video clips with me that met me in some dark places. The videos *See It Through, How to Be Brave* by Steven Furtick, *Going Beyond Ministries – The Multitude* by Priscilla Shirer, and *It Had to Happen* by Steven Furtick, landed me bowed down on my face in worship. Thank you, Vee! Veirdre's relationship with Abba Father and obedience to send me the video clips as she was led was imperative to my desperate search for answers. It was not only timely, but those answers provided the clarity I needed moving forward and a timely reminder I too was empowered, resilient and uniquely inspiring.

When we remain faithful, fearless, and fabulous we can look at the faces of our haters, challenges, and adversity and hold our heads high.

We can overcome while being resilient despite what we experience as women who are mothers, grandmothers, sisters, aunts and daughters. I want you to look at every challenge you have faced, may be facing, or will face and know that you are carrying greatness within you. Sometimes the weight of that greatness may feel uncomfortable due to the circumstances of life. These challenges can be family hardships, fear, guilt, economic struggles, low self-esteem, sense of worthlessness and abandonment. Don't let these circumstances withhold you from releasing the greatness inside of you. Instead, erase every lie ever told to you and replace those lies with a tenacious resolve that leaves YOU standing on only the TRUTH. Replace the lie of lack, which can lead to hopelessness. YOU have enough, YOU are enough, and YOU are good enough! Replace the lie of fear within YOU and operate out of a spirit of love, power and a sound mind! Replace the lie of abandonment and replace it with the truth YOU are never alone for the Master is always present! MOST importantly, the ULTIMATE truth is that YOU are fearfully, wonderfully and marvelously made in the image of Abba Father!

Women know without a shadow of doubt - YOU are

FIERCE and FABULOUS!

Resilient Affirmation

I acknowledge that I AM POWERFUL

I acknowledge that I AM EXTRAORDINARY

I acknowledge that I AM AUTHENTIC

I acknowledge that I AM RESILIENT

I acknowledge that I AM GOOD ENOUGH

REFLECTION ACTIVITY

According to Psalms 139:14, what is your interpretation of being fear fully and wonderfully made?

_____

_____

_____

_____

_____

What was YOUR greatest self-defeating belief YOU had to overcome that was significant to unleashing your personal greatness?

_____

_____

_____

_____

_____

_____

_____

My personal empowerment chapter reflection...

_____

_____

_____

_____

_____

_____

_____

_____

_____

_____

_____

_____

_____

_____

_____

_____

_____

_____

_____

_____

_____

_____

_____

_____

_____

_____

_____

_____

_____

_____

_____

_____

_____

_____

Chapter 8

Reflections of Gratitude

Each day is an opportunity to express gratefulness. As you maintain its importance, continue to appreciate this wonderful and inspiring journey of practicing gratitude.

Be grateful for what you have and you will end up with more. If you focus on what you don't have, you will always feel that you don't have enough.

Gratitude is captivating an image of an exceptional life experience and storing is as one of the treasures of your heart.

A paradigm shift in our beliefs from one of expectation to one of gratitude can change our entire atmosphere.

Gratitude unravels the abundance of life. Gratitude provides wisdom of our past, peace in our now moments and a manifestation of our vision for the future.

A grateful soul understands that one of the greatest purposes of life is to love it, to fully appreciate every life experience, and to eagerly pursue our dreams absent of fear for fresher and more abundance.

Resilient Affirmation

I acknowledge that I AM POWERFUL

I acknowledge that I AM EXTRAORDINARY

I acknowledge that I AM AUTHENTIC

I acknowledge that I AM RESILIENT

I acknowledge that I AM GOOD ENOUGH

REFLECTION ACTIVITY

1. Start a Gratitude Journal

2. Each night write down three things you are grateful for.

3. Use the power of gratitude whenever you find yourself in a life challenges.

My personal empowerment mantra is…

_____

_____

_____

_____

_____

_____

_____

_____

_____

_____

_____

_____

_____

_____

_____

_____

As you continue to express a heart of gratitude for what you have,

you open yourself to experience abundance.

Notes

"It is this belief in a power larger than myself and other than myself, which allows me to venture into the unknown and even the unknowable". Maya Angelou. (n.d.). Great-Quotes.com. Retrieved Thu Sep 7 20:31:00 2017, from Great-Quotes.com Web site: http://www.great-quotes.com/quote/

"We receive His peace when we ask Him for it. We keep His peace by extending it to others. Those are the keys and there are no others." "Marianne Williamson Quotes." Quotes.net. STANDS4 LLC, 2017. Web. 7 Sep. 2017.
<http://www.quotes.net/authors/Marianne+Williamson>.

"Courage is the most important of all the virtues, because without courage you can't practice any other virtue consistently. You can practice any virtue erratically, but nothing consistently without courage." Maya Angelou. (n.d.). Great-Quotes.com. Retrieved Thu Sep 7 20:31:00 2017, from Great-Quotes.com Web site: http://www.great-quotes.com/quote/

"Invest in the human soul. Who knows, it may be a diamond in the rough." Jone Johnson Lewis. "Mary McLeod Bethune Quotes." About Women's History. URL:

http://womenshistory.about.com/od/quotes/a/mary_bethune.htm .
"I Didn't Know My Own Strength [Daddy's Groove Magic Island Radio Mix] Lyrics." Lyrics.com. STANDS4 LLC, 2017. Web. 8 Sep. 2017.
<https://www.lyrics.com/lyric/17888712>.

"Woman of Destiny [So.Be.It.Entertainment] Lyrics."
http://www.cduniverse.com/productinfo.asp?pid=9940196

"WOMAN OF DESTINY"

Lyrics: Linda Brown, Cheryl Hurley, Pam Nichols, Shelly Pullian
and Cheryl Nichols.
Music: Shelly B. Pullian, Pamela E. Nichols
Written: November 2001

A woman of destiny, that's who I long to be
Fulfilled, satisfied, ready for the world to see
A woman of destiny, that's who I long to be
Knowing that I am the woman I'm destined to be.

I'm determined to stay on course as you are guiding me
And if trials and struggles cause me to question, to
question I'll remember the peace and the pleasure that a
life of purpose brings.

A woman of destiny, that's who I long to be
Fulfilled, satisfied, ready for the world to see
A woman of destiny, that's who I long to be
Knowing I am the woman I'm destined to be.

No more doubts and no fears will swallow my dreams
So the vision for my life stays so clear, so clear
Cause you formed me, you made me, you gave me
The will to be free, to be me

Teach me, show me, help me to know
Just what I should do and where I should go.

A woman of destiny, that's who I long to be
Fulfilled, satisfied, ready for the world to see
A woman of destiny, that's who I long to be
Knowing that I am the woman I'm destined to be.

*Song available for MP3 download purchase at
http://www.cduniverse.com/productinfo.asp?pid=9940196

Healing in all areas-- emotionally, mentally, physically and spiritually is a very important step to enjoying a fulfilling life.

Cheryl A.S. Hurley is an extraordinary woman who embraces her life's mission wholeheartedly. A certified Life coach with a passion for tapping potential and maximizing prospects, she creates an open and safe space for clients to clarify intentions, expand possibilities and reach new heights. Cheryl coaches women to conquer their fears, achieve their dreams and realize their unique purpose despite the circumstances they may have faced.

This is accomplished through a three-step process where she empowers, inspires and cultivates individuals into firm and capable leaders. She displays strength of character in areas of administration and organizational communication, and at workshops/seminars, she never fails to impart positively. She combines honesty and empathy and attendees have repeatedly testified her coaching sessions are inspiring, energetic and transformative.

"I candidly recall being a classic human being with my very own struggles and stories to tell." She says, *"My ongoing journey of personal discovery happened while on my committed journey of helping others. It took me several years to overcome depression and have a change in mindset and beliefs. I worked hard, sought the support of others and wholeheartedly embraced the hope that my struggles would result in something valuable to help others."*

She conducts individual and group coaching and leads workshops throughout Philadelphia and the surrounding area.

"The legacy that a woman leaves is the one she lives, breathes and walks."

79

For more information, please visit:

www.livingstrongconsultingLLC.com

Email: churley@livingstrongllc.com or

Empowered2InspireYOU@gmail.com

(267) 499-3747

Made in the USA
Middletown, DE
31 October 2023

41677320R00046